SONGS OF THE 1900's

PIANO • VOCAL • GUITAR

THE DECADE SERIES

1900-1909

P9-DME-782

ISBN 0-7935-3125-X

HAL•LEONARD™
CORPORATION

7777 W. BLUEMOUND RD. P.O. BOX 13819 MILWAUKEE, WI 53213

Copyright ©1994 by HAL LEONARD CORPORATION
International Copyright Secured   All Rights Reserved

The 1900's (1900-1909)

by Elaine Schmidt

As the Twentieth Century dawned, Americans looked to the future with breathless anticipation. Although few could have imagined what wonders the new century would reveal, all agreed that it promised economic growth, technological advancement and an ever increasing standard of living. By the end of the decade, the automobile had become a fixture on American roads, telephone and railroad networks expanded to connect distant cities, and the Wright brothers, Kitty Hawk well behind them, were winging through the Ohio skies. While Einstein's Theory of Relativity and Max Planck's Quantum Theory made news, Americans were entranced by inventions which altered their daily lives. As the safety razor freed men from full beards, the motor washing machine ended scrub-board drudgery for women. The mechanical pencil, subway, and hot running water held far more interest than the first radio sound broadcast. Women were consumed with achieving the wistful Gibson girl look, and driving clothes became the obsession of the motorized set.

In virtual obscurity Orville and Wilbur Wright make their historic first flight at Kitty Hawk, North Carolina, 1903.

The look, sound and taste of America changed with the waves of immigrants that passed through Ellis Island. They brought with them a world of music, languages, foods, fashions, religions and culture. From the immigrants came delicatessens, kindergartens, bon bons, kaiser rolls and pasta. Fighting for their rights, they organized labor unions and demanded 8-hour works days and child labor laws. They brought political ideas that would shape the country, forming the Populist and Socialist political parties. The immigrants also brought their children, the likes of Irving Berlin and George Gershwin.

In 1901, a shocked nation grieved the assassination of President McKinley. The rough-riding Teddy Roosevelt roared into the White House with six boisterous children in tow. Roosevelt sided with workers, was unafraid of big business and protected the National forests. He coined phrases that came to define the era, referring to exposé journalists of

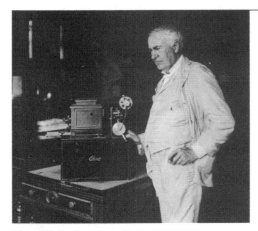

Edison and his phonograph. He believed it to be primarily for business use, but by the early years of the century he knew his favorite invention would be primarily used for entertainment.

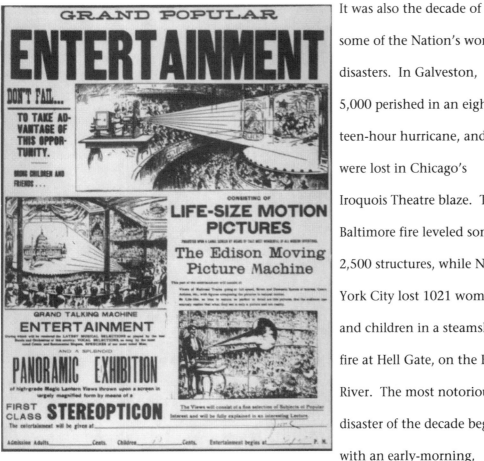

the day as "muckrakers," attacking illegal businesses in an act of "trust–busting," and noting that he preferred to "Speak softly and carry a big stick." Roosevelt's Big Stick policy was demonstrated to the world when he dispatched the 16 white battleships of the U.S. fleet, to sail around the world. Their year-long voyage quietly established America as a world power with which to be reckoned.

It was also the decade of some of the Nation's worst disasters. In Galveston, 5,000 perished in an eighteen-hour hurricane, and 602 were lost in Chicago's Iroquois Theatre blaze. The Baltimore fire leveled some 2,500 structures, while New York City lost 1021 women and children in a steamship fire at Hell Gate, on the East River. The most notorious disaster of the decade began with an early-morning, muted rumble. San Francisco awakened on April 6, 1906 to the infamous earthquake, which ignited a three-day, raging

inferno. When the smoke cleared, 450 people had died, 490 city blocks were in ashes, 225,000 people left homeless and 25,000 buildings were in ruins. The country rushed to send aid. Funds came from Washington, D.C., free bread from Los Angeles, one day's ticket revenues from the Philadelphia Athletics and so on. When foreign nations offered help, President Roosevelt respectfully declined, saying that the country would "...show the world that under such an adversity the United States would take care of its own..." The ashes had barely cooled when reconstruction began on "a metropolis finer than Paris."

In the fledgling entertainment industry, the Victor Talking machine was playing wax cylinders, and moving picture shows were amazing audiences. The country was reading Mark Twain, Jack London, Theodore Dresser and Edith Wharton, and flocking to hear Enrico Caruso at the Metropolitan Opera. Silent films offered "The Great Train Robbery," while John Barrymore enthralled theater audiences. Nostalgia tugged at American hearts, carrying William F. Cody, better known as

Buffalo Bill, to the height of his popularity. His touring Wild West Show romanticized the cowboy west. Black Elk, Calamity Jane, Annie Oakley and a host of livestock toured with him, their real wild west having faded into history.

Vaudeville and the Ziegfeld Follies drew crowds. Broadway was fast becoming the theatrical center of the country. The hot shows of the decade included *Florodora* (1900), a British import featuring the double sextet, "Tell Me Pretty Maiden," and *The Wizard of Oz* (1903), in which Dorothy and her pet cow were blown to Oz. Franz Lehàr's Viennese operetta *The Merry Widow* (1907), produced the hit songs "Maxim's," "Vilia," and "I Love You So (The Merry Widow Waltz)." It also sparked fashion trends of Merry Widow hats, corsets, dresses and cigarettes. Also from Vienna, *The Chocolate Soldier* (1909) included the standard, "My Hero." Victor Herbert became a household name. His *Babes in Toyland*

(1903) included the hits "Toyland" and "March of the Toys," while *Mlle. Modiste* (1905) featured "I Want What I Want When I Want It." *The Red Mill* (1906) gave the country "Moonbeams" and "Every Day Is Ladies Day With Me."

Grand Old Flag," and "Give My Regards to Broadway." Vaudeville and the Follies offered their share of successful tunes as evidenced by "School Days" (1907), "Shine on Harvest Moon," (1908), "On the Road to Mandalay."

And then there was George M. Cohan, the brash, versatile, young, song dance man from a family of performers. Moving from vaude-ville to Broadway, Cohan pro-vided music, lyrics and book for *Little Johnny Jones* (1904) and *Forty–Five Minutes from Broadway* (1906). His hit songs of the decade included "Harrigan," "Mary's a Grand Old Name," "Yankee Doodle Boy," "You're a

A scene from Victor Herbert's 1905 operetta Mlle. Modiste.

Pianos were fixtures in most American homes, where an evening's entertainment often included group singing of popular songs. Barbershop quartets crooned such hits as "Sweet Adeline" (1903) and "Wait Till the Sun Shines Nellie" (1905). The decade's hit songs were waltzes, ballads, event songs, love songs or the new ragtime tunes. A successful song often became a trademark piece for a star, moving from show to show with the performer. Blanche Ring introduced "I've Got Rings on My Fingers" (1909) in *The Midnight Sons* (1909), taking it to *The Yankee Girl* (1910), *When Claudia Smiles* (1914) and *Right This Way* (1938) and singing it until the end of her career.

Ragtime, the emerging rage, included hits such as "Under the Bamboo Tree" (1902), "Bill Bailey" (1902) and "The Entertainer (1902)." Dialect songs were also popular. In black dialect, "Mighty Lak a Rose" (1901) and "What You "Goin' to Do When the Rent Comes 'Round?" became hits. Scottish dialect tunes, notably "She Is Ma Daisy" and "Stop Yer Tickling, Jock!," had their day. Tunes were imported from Europe and altered to American taste. "It's Delightful to be Married" (1907) was a French popular song, while "Glow Worm" (1902) first appeared in Germany as "Glüwürmchen."

The banquet marking the formation of US Steel in 1901, with eight firms merging.

"Because" (1902) and "Has Anybody Seen Kelly?" (1909) migrated from England. "From the popular minstrel shows came "Ida, Sweet as Apple Cider" (1903) and similar songs came from the popular minstrel shows of day.

A good song did not need a show to become a success. The sentimental ballad "A Bird in a Gilded Cage" (1900), was a success in its own right, selling over 2 million copies. After "In the Shade of the Old Apple Tree" became a hit, it was added to *The Rogers Brothers in Ireland* (1905). Nor did a song have to appear in New York to gain fame. "I Wonder Who's Kissing Her Now" (1909) appeared in *The Prince of Tonight* (1909) in Chicago and *Miss Nobody from*

Starland (1910) in Milwaukee. Other songs just couldn't be ignored. "In the Good Old Summertime" (1902) was turned down by publishers leery of seasonal songs. Blanche Ring included it in *The Defender* (1902), which brought it phenomenal success. As late as 1949, the song was the basis for an MGM film

Powerful tycoon John D. Rockefeller, America's first billionaire and founder of Standard Oil, in a 1900 cartoon with the caption, "What a funny little government." Many charged at the time that he had the White House in one pocket and Congress in the other.

A satiric cartoon from 1907, with the note "$400,000,000 will be spent in Europe by American tourists this season. While immigration was at its peak from Europe, well-heeled Americans were also crossing the Atlantic in record numbers.

of the same name. "Anchors Away" (1906) was written for the annual Army-Navy football game—the next year the U.S. Fleet set sail. It was adopted as the song of the U.S. Navy. "Take Me Out to the Ball Game," (1908) quickly became the unofficial anthem for America's national game. Event songs recounted the news of the decade. "Casey Jones" (1909) immortalized the fallen railroad hero, while "Meet Me in St. Louis, Louis" (1904) was inspired by the St. Louis Exposition.

One of the first educational institutions to espouse the cause of black Americans was the Hampton Institute, founded in 1881. Here is a group of women graduates from the class of 1906 at the school's 25th anniversary celebration.

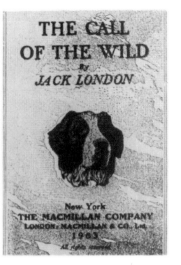

Jack London, the most popular author of his era, had a major success with the 1903 novel *The Call of the Wild*, an adventure story about the Klondike gold-rush days in the last years of the 19th century.

As the decade closed, it was clear that Broadway musicals were here to stay and that entertainment was a burgeoning industry. In 1909, Victor produced historic recordings of Nora Bayes singing "Has Anybody Seen Kelly?" and Blanche Ring performing "Yip-I-Addy-I-Ay!." The age of phonographs was beginning. Soon Victrolas and radios would find their way into most American homes. Not far into the future, the world would be plunged into the first of many devastating conflicts. Left behind with the charm of the parlor piano and upbeat popular songs was an age of national innocence.

ANCHORS AWEIGH

Words by ALFRED HART MILES and R. LOVELL
Music by CHARLES A. ZIMMERMAN

ASK HER WHILE THE BAND IS PLAYING

Lyric by GLEN MAC DONOUGH
Music by VICTOR HERBERT

While the cel-lo sweet and mel-low aids the win - some

(Cello)

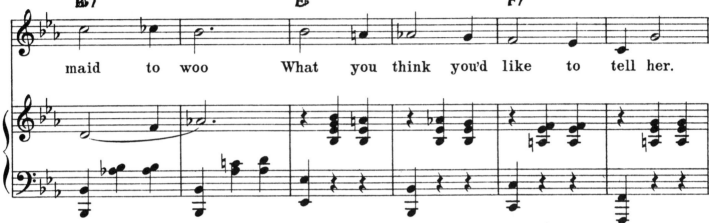

maid to woo What you think you'd like to tell her.

Let the soul - ful o - boe play Ask her while the

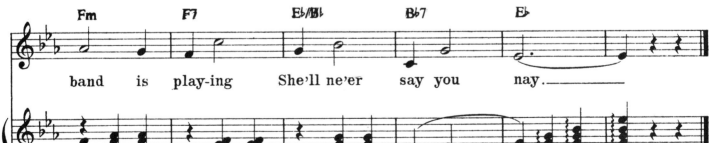

band is play-ing She'll ne'er say you nay._____

AT DAWNING
(I LOVE YOU)

NELLE RICHMOND EBERHART
CHARLES WAKEFIELD CADMAN
Op. 29, No. 1
French by SUZANNE d'ASTORIA JACKOWSKA

BECAUSE

Words by EDWARD TESCHEMACHER
Music by GUY D' HARDELOT

BILL BAILEY

Words and Music by
HUGHIE CANNON

A BIRD IN A GILDED CAGE

Words by ARTHUR J. LAMB
Music by HARRY VON TILZER

*) Symbols for Guitar, Chords for Ukulele and Banjo

BON BON BUDDY
(BON BON BABY)

Words by ALEX ROGERS
Music by WILL MARION COOK

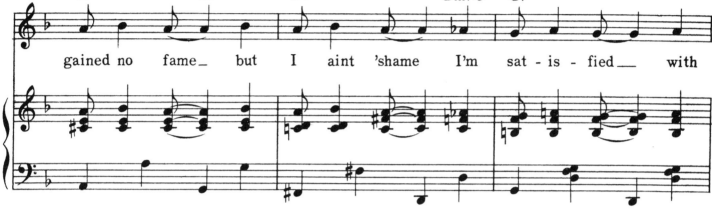

BY THE LIGHT OF THE SILVERY MOON

Words by EDWARD MADDEN
Music by GUS EDWARDS

By the light _____ of the sil - ver - y moon _____ I want to spoon. _____ To my hon - ey I'll croon love's tune. Hon - ey

CASEY JONES

Lyrics by T. LAWRENCE SEIBERT
Music by EDDIE NEWTON

Moderato

1. Come all you round-ers if you want to hear a
2. Put in your wa-ter and sho-vel in your coal put your
3. Ca-sey pulled up that Re-no hill he
4. Ca-sey said just be-fore he died there's

sto-ry a-bout a brave En-gi-neer
heat out the win-dow watch them driv-ers roll I'll
toot-ed for the cross-ing with an aw-ful shrill The
two more roads that I'd like to ride

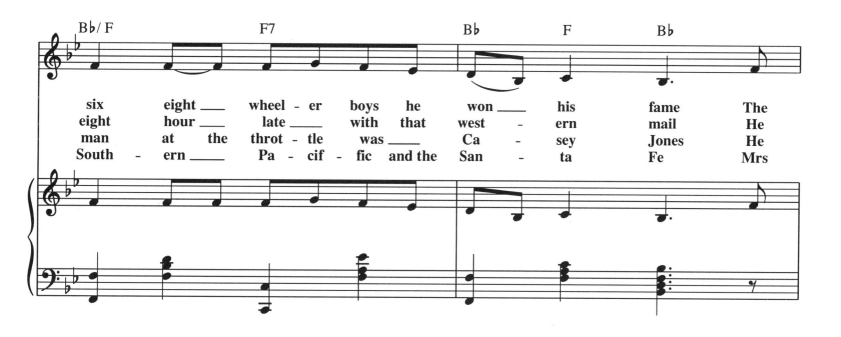

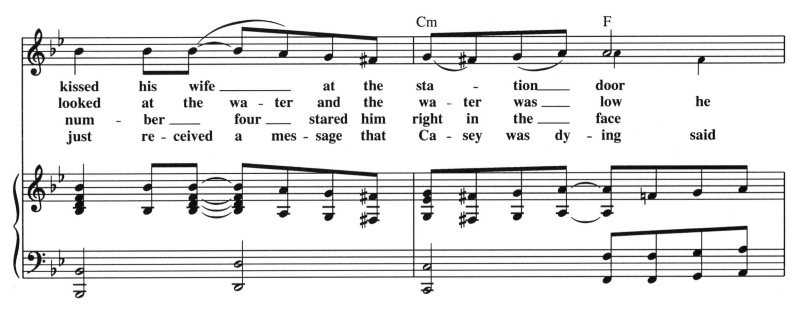

kissed his wife _____ at the sta - tion _____ door
looked at the wa - ter and the wa - ter was _____ low he
num - ber _____ four _____ stared him right in the _____ face
just re - ceived a mes - sage that Ca - sey was dy - ing said

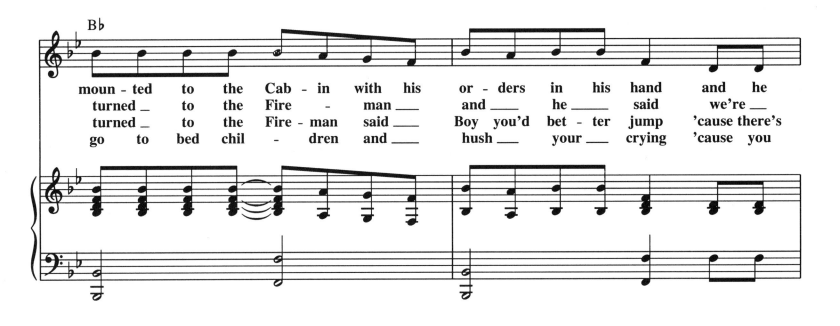

moun - ted to the Cab - in with his or - ders in his hand and he
turned _ to the Fire - man _____ and _____ he _____ said we're _____
turned _ to the Fire - man said _____ Boy you'd bet - ter jump 'cause there's
go to bed chil - dren and _____ hush _____ your _____ crying 'cause you

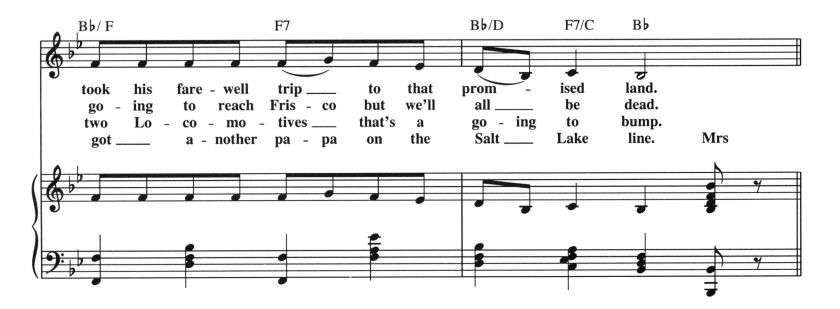

took his fare - well trip _____ to that prom - ised land.
go - ing to reach Fris - co but we'll all _____ be dead.
two Lo - co - mo - tives _____ that's a go - ing to bump.
got _____ a - nother pa - pa on the Salt _____ Lake line. Mrs

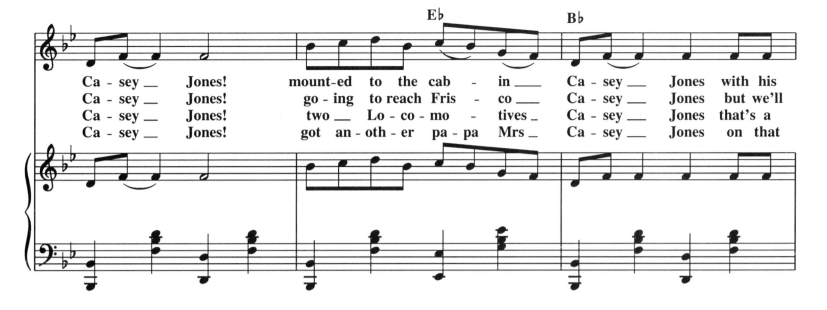

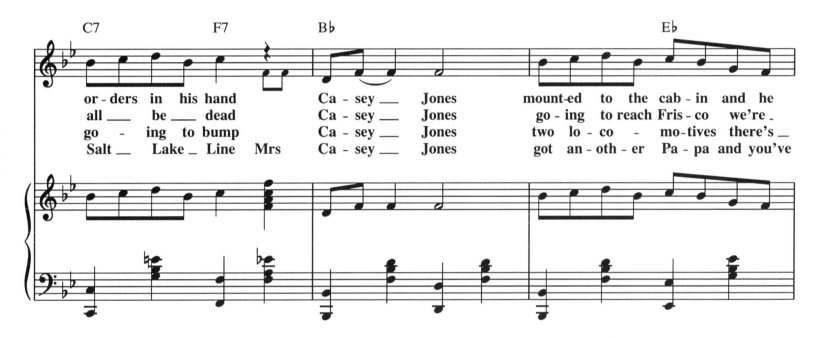

D.C. to vamp.

CUDDLE UP A LITTLE CLOSER,
LOVEY MINE

Lyric by O. A. HAUERBACH
Music by KARL HOSCHNA

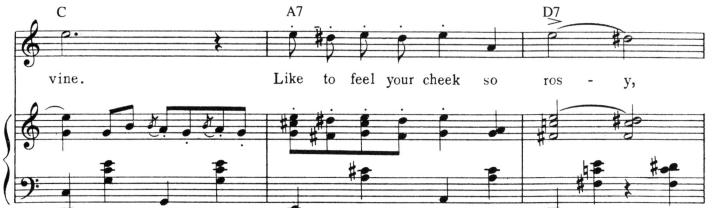

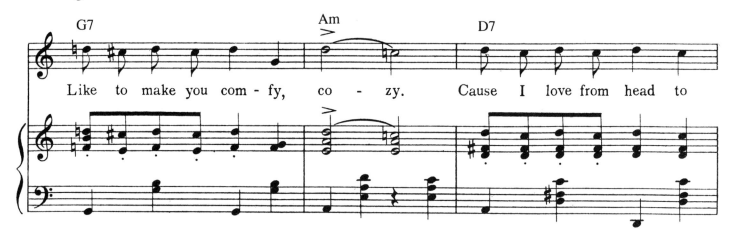

EVERY DAY IS LADIES' DAY WITH ME

Words by HENRY BLOSSOM
Music by VICTOR HERBERT

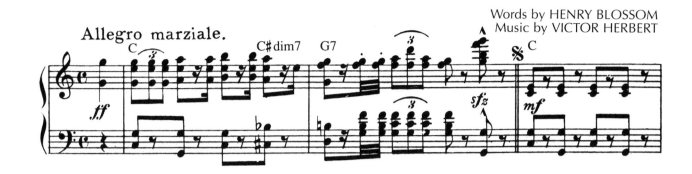

I should like, with-out un-due re-it-er-a-tion of the e-go, To ex-
It's a frightfull thing to think of all the hearts that I have broken, Al-tho'

plain, how ve-ry hard I find it is to make my pay go 'Round a-
each one fell in love with me with-out the slight-est to-ken, That my

mong my vul-gar cred-it-ors I'm fear-ful-ly in debt, For I al-ways have af-ford-ed an-y-
fa-tal gift of beau-ty had in-flamed her lit-tle heart, But I found that some small fa-vor al-ways

44

THE ENTERTAINER

By SCOTT JOPLIN

FASCINATION
(VALSE TZIGANE)

By F.D. MARCHETTI

Flowing Waltz

FROM THE LAND OF SKY BLUE WATER

CHARLES WAKEFIELD CADMAN
Opus 45, No. 1
Poem by NELLE RICHMOND EBERHART
Omaha Tribal Melodies collected by
ALICE C. FLETCHER

*Flageolet Love Call of the Omahas

maid; _____ And her eyes they are

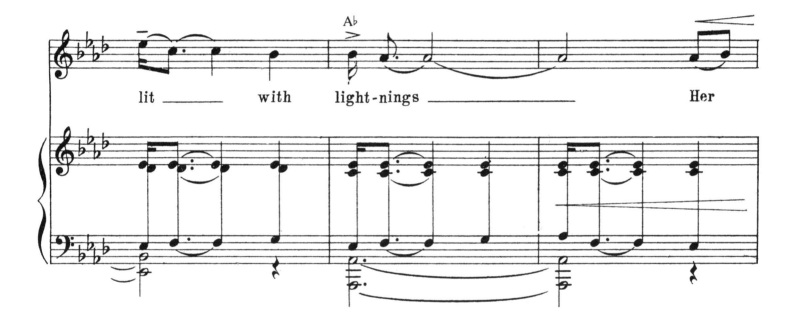

lit ____ with light-nings _____ Her

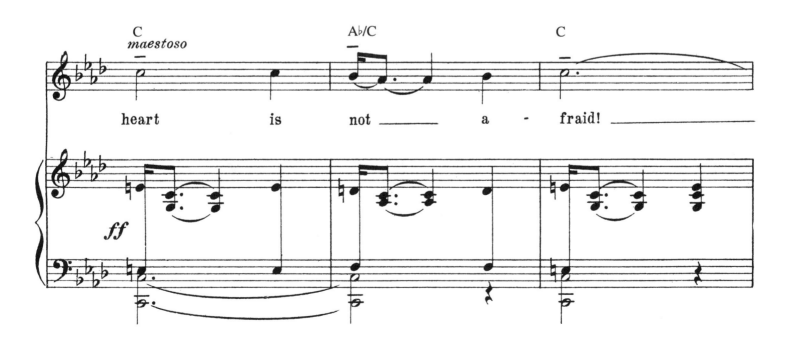

heart is not ____ a - fraid! _____

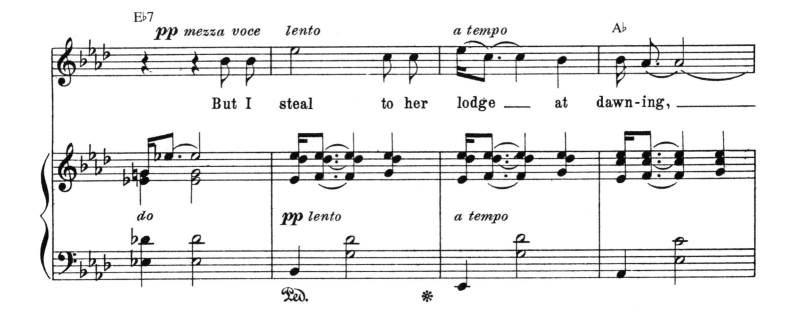

She is sick for the Sky - blue Wa - ter,

The cap - tive maid is mute.

GIVE MY REGARDS TO BROADWAY

Words and Music by
GEORGE M. COHAN

GLOW WORM

Music by PAUL LINCKE
Words by LILLA CAYLEY ROBINSON

When the night falls si-lent-ly,___ the night falls si-lent-ly___ on for-ests
"Lit - tle glow-worm, tell me pray,___ oh glow-worm, tell me pray,___ how did you

dream - ing, Lov - ers wan - der forth to see,___ they wan-der
kin - dle, Lamps that by the break of day,___ that by the

forth to see___ the bright stars gleam - ing; And lest they should
break of day,___ must fade and dwin - dle?" "Ah this se - cret,

HARRIGAN

Words and Music by
GEORGE M. COHAN

HAS ANYBODY HERE SEEN KELLY?

Words and Music by C.W. MURPHY, WILL LETTERS,
JOHN CHARLES MOORE and WILLIAM J. McKENNA

I HEAR YOU CALLING ME

Words by HAROLD HARFORD
Music by CHARLES MARSHALL

I LOVE YOU TRULY

Words and Music by
CARRIE JACOBS-BOND

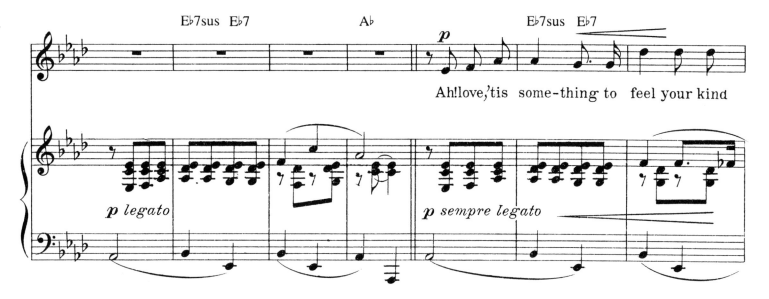

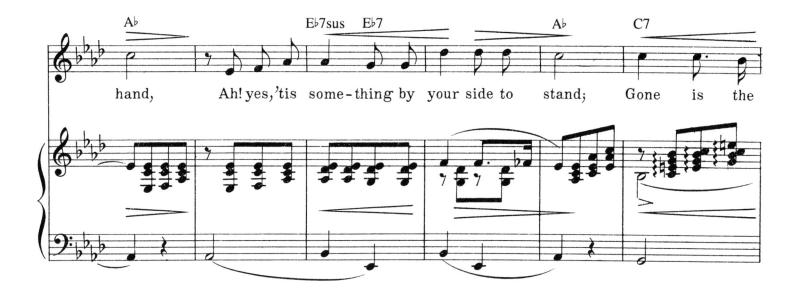

I LOVE, I LOVE, I LOVE MY WIFE, BUT OH YOU KID

Words by JIMMY LUCAS
Music by HARRY VON TILZER

I WONDER WHO'S KISSING HER NOW

Lyric by HOUGH & ADAMS
Music by JOS. E. HOWARD

true; _____ You have kissed 'neath the moon while the world seemed in
pressed; _____ But the world moves a - pace and the loves of to -

tune, Then you've left her to hunt a new game, ___ Does it ev- er oc-
day Flit a - way with a smile and a tear, ___ So you nev- er can

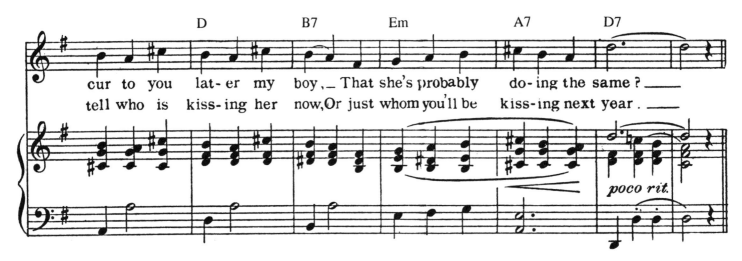

cur to you lat- er my boy,_ That she's probably do- ing the same? ___
tell who is kiss-ing her now, Or just whom you'll be kiss-ing next year. ___

poco rit.

Chorus. G

I won-der who's kiss-ing her now, _____ Won-der who's teach-ing her

dolce. *p -f*

now, _____ Won-der who's look-ing in-to her eyes Breath-ing

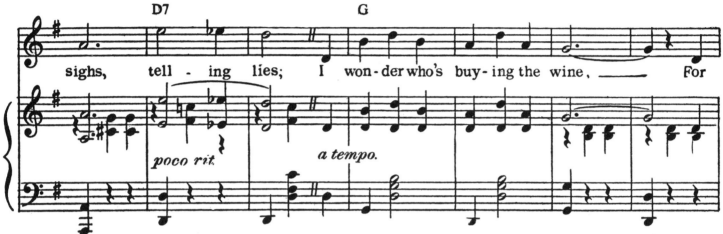

sighs, tell-ing lies; I won-der who's buy-ing the wine, _____ For

poco rit.   *a tempo.*

lips that I used to call mine. _____ Won-der if she ev-er tells him of

allargamente.

me, I won-der who's kissing her now. _____ I kiss-ing her now _____

f   *rall.*   *p*   *a tempo.*

I WANT WHAT I WANT
WHEN I WANT IT

Lyric by HENRY BLOSSOM
Music by VICTOR HERBERT

I'M AFRAID TO COME HOME IN THE DARK

Words by HARRY WILLIAMS
Music by EGBERT VAN ALSTYNE

1. "Jones-ie" mar-ried Ma-bel, a wise old owl was he,___ He told his wife he nev-er drank a strong-er thing than tea,___ But
2. That night af-ter din-ner, he bade his wife a - dieu,___ Said she "Oh no, its dark and so I'm goin' to go with you",___ But
3. She kissed him good morning, to _ see him she. was glad,___ And when she tucked him up in bed says Jones "I guess I'm bad"___ Next

I'VE GOT RINGS ON MY FINGERS
(A/K/A MUMBO, JUMBO JIJJIBOO J. O'SHEA)

Words by WESTON and BARNES
Music by MAURICE SCOTT

1. Jim O-'Shea was cast a-way Up-on an In-dian isle, The
2. O'er the sea went Rose Mc Gee To see her na-bob grand, He
3. Em-'rald green he robed his queen, To share with him his throne, 'Mid

na-tives there they lik'd his hair, They lik'd his I-rish smile, So
sat with-in his pal-an-quin, And when she'd kissed his hand, He
eas-tern charms and wav-ing palms, They'd sham-rocks, I-rish grown, Sent

Chorus.

"Sure, I've got rings on my fin-gers, bells on my toes,

El-e-phants to ride up-on, my lit-tle I-rish Rose, So

come to your na-bob, and next Pat-rick's Day, Be

Mis-tress Mum-bo Jum-bo Jij-ji-boo J. O-'Shea. "Sure I've got Shea."

IDA, SWEET AS APPLE CIDER

Lyric by EDDIE LEONARD
Music by EDDIE MUNSON

IN THE GOOD OLD SUMMERTIME

Words by REN SHIELDS
Music by GEORGE EVANS

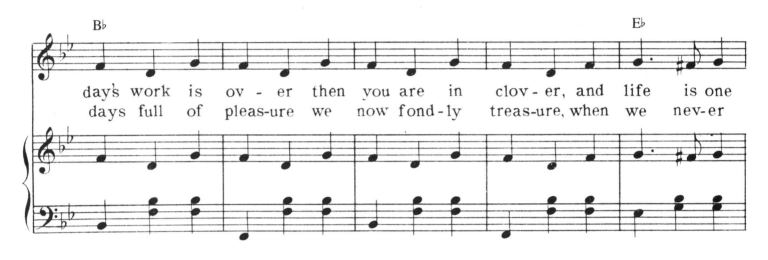

CHORUS.

In the good old sum-mer time, _____ In the good old sum-mer time, _____

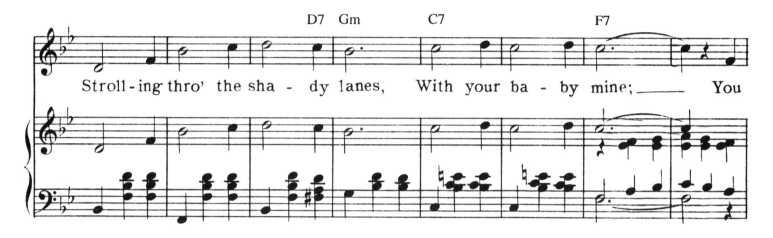

Stroll-ing thro' the sha - dy lanes, With your ba - by mine; _____ You

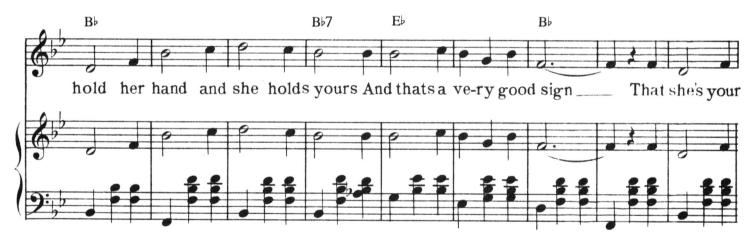

hold her hand and she holds yours And thats a ve-ry good sign _____ That she's your

toot-sey wootsey in The good old sum-mer time. _____ In the time. _____

IT'S DELIGHTFUL TO BE MARRIED

Words by ANNA HELD
Music by V. SCOTTO

In our schooldays,— mer-ry school-days,— We were hap-py girls and boys;—— We would al-ways play to-geth-er,—— And our

Soon we mar-ried,— you and I, dear,— You to me and I to you,—— And we had a lit-tle home, dear,—— With just

When old age comes, to us both, dear,— We will still be in the game;—— I will be a gay old par-ty,—— You will

Chorus.

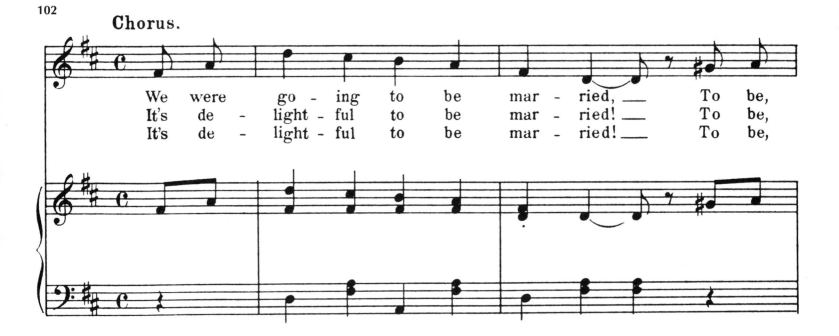

We were go - ing to be mar - ried, ___ To be,
It's de - light - ful to be mar - ried! ___ To be,
It's de - light - ful to be mar - ried! ___ To be,

to be,- to be, to be,- to be mar - ried, ___ When we old - er grew and
to be,- to be, to be,- to be mar - ried! ___ There is noth - ing half so
to be,- to be, to be,- to be mar - ried! ___ For the heart won't be un -

bold - er, Then a lit - tle while we tar - ried, When I
jol - ly, As a hap - py wed - ded life; ___ And I
ru - ly, If it real - ly loves one tru - ly; And your

IN THE SHADE OF THE OLD APPLE TREE

Words by HARRY H. WILLIAMS
Music by EGBERT VAN ALSTYNE

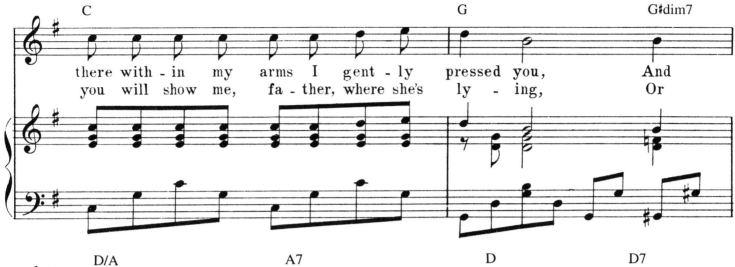

there with-in my arms I gent-ly pressed you, And
you will show me, fa-ther, where she's ly-ing, Or

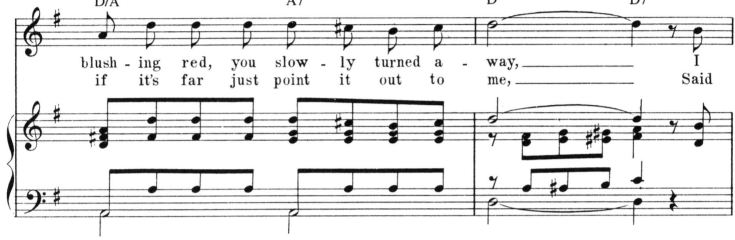

blush-ing red, you slow-ly turned a-way, _____ I
if it's far just point it out to me, _____ Said

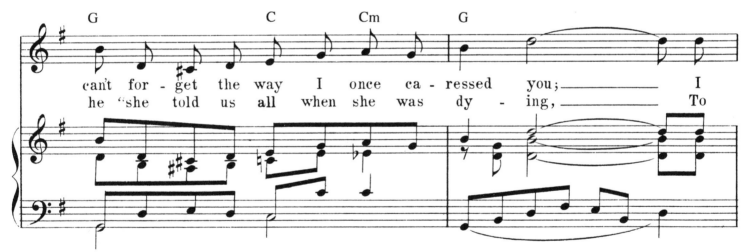

can't for-get the way I once ca-ressed you; _____ I
he "she told us all when she was dy-ing, _____ To

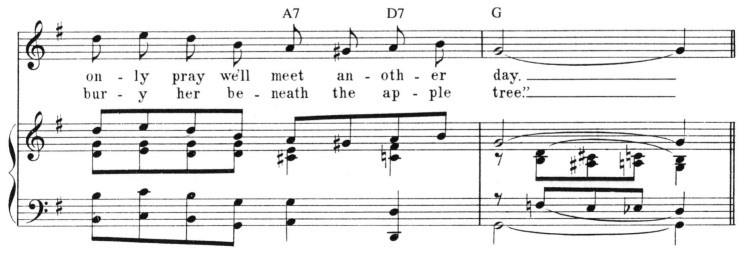

on-ly pray we'll meet an-oth-er day. _____
bur-y her be-neath the ap-ple tree."_____

LOVE IS LIKE A CIGARETTE

Lyric by GLEN MAC DONOUGH
Music by VICTOR HERBERT

in - cense mounts___ In swirl - ing curves a - bove,___ And as I
- witch - ing shades!___ Each sad - ly smiles at me,___ With each I

dream, My fan - cy turns to Love!___
swore, To love e - ter - nal - ly!___

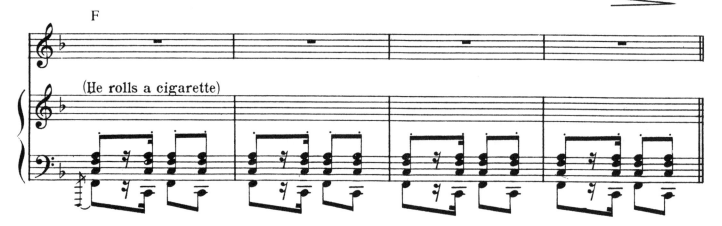

(He rolls a cigarette)

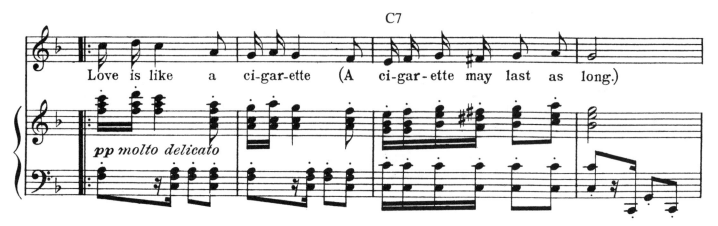

Love is like a ci-gar-ette (A ci-gar-ette may last as long.)

pp molto delicato

Light-ed at a heart a-flame For a time it's fire is strong.

Fra-grant clouds then from us veil Ev-'ry sor - row ev-'ry

doubt, Till we wake at last to find. That our

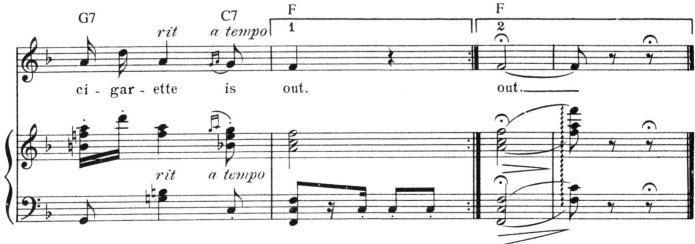

ci - gar - ette is out. out.

JUST W-WEARYIN' FOR YOU

Words by FRANK STANTON
Music by CARRIE JACOBS-BOND

Moderato

2. Morn - in' comes, the birds a - wake,

Used to sing so for your sake But there's sad-ness

in the notes That come trill - in' from their throats. Seem to feel your

ab-sence, too, Just a-wear-y - in' for you.

D. S. al Fine

MARCH OF THE TOYS

With Spirit

By VICTOR HERBERT

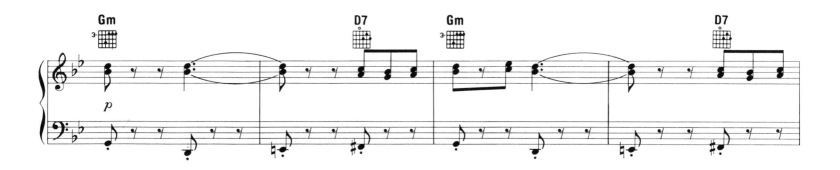

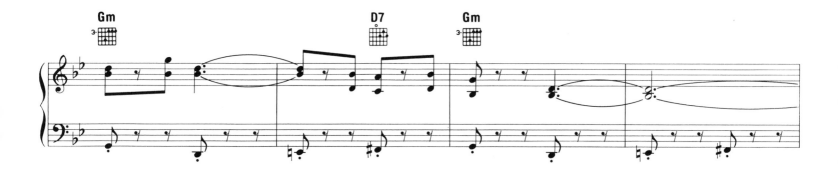

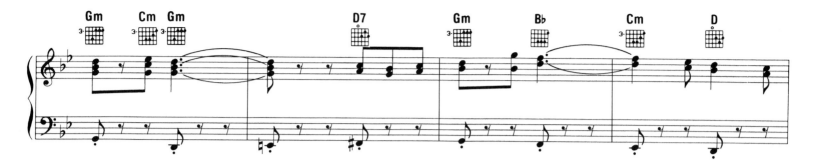

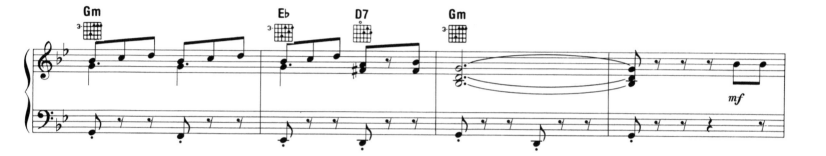

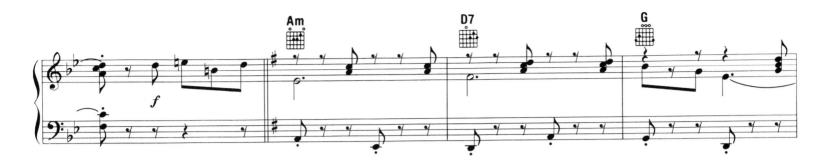

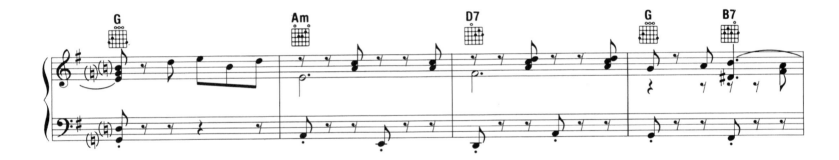

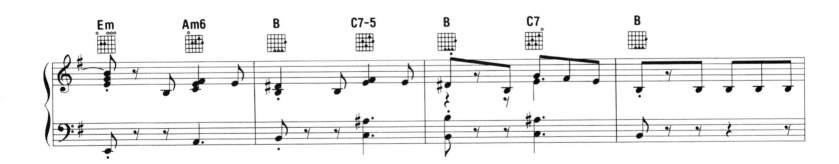

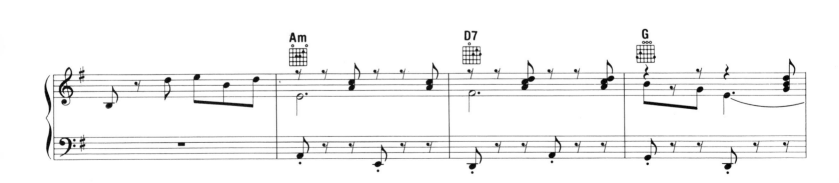

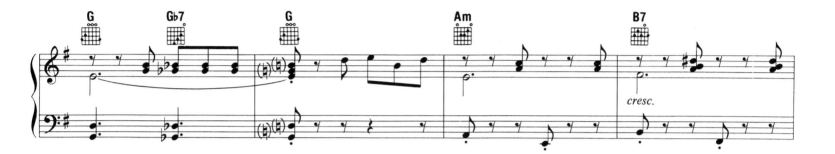

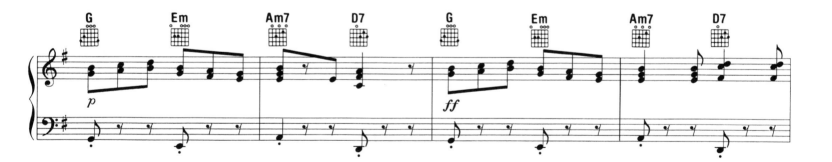

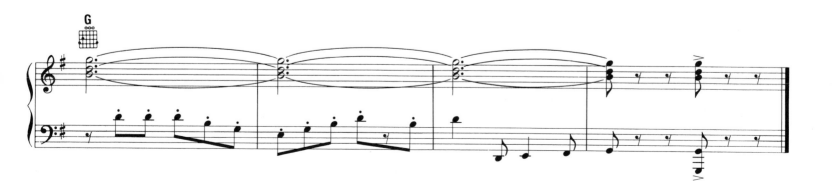

MARY'S A GRAND OLD NAME

By GEORGE M. COHAN

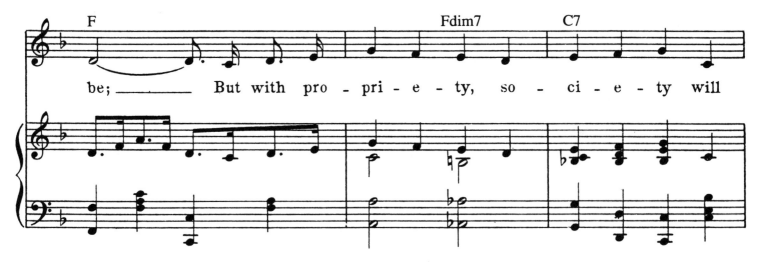

MAXIM'S

German Lyrics by VICTOR LEON and LEO STEIN
Music by FRANZ LEHÁR
Translations by GEORGE BONIFACE

Fa-ther-land you cause by day a lot of trou-ble and dis-may, But
Va-ter-land, du machst bei Tag mir schon ge-nü-gend Müh' und Plag'!

night leads me, a dip-lo-mat, to serve my-self, I'm good at that! For
Nacht braucht je-der Di-plo-mat doch mei-sten-teils für sich pri-vat! Um

cheeks glow like the rose;   and what a pleas-ure this is, to
häu - fig can - ca - niert,   und geht's an's Ko - sen, Küs - sen mit

share a lot of kiss - es! Lo - lo, Do - do, Jou - jou,   Clo -
al - len die - sen Süs - sen: Lo - lo, Do - do, Jou - jou,   Clo -

clo, Mar - got, Frou - frou;   No won - der I'm for - get - ting that
clo, Mar - got, Frou - frou,   dann kann ich leicht ver - ges - sen das

Allegro.

dear old Fa - ther-land!
teu' - re Va - ter-land.

MEET ME IN ST. LOUIS, LOUIS

Words by ANDREW B. STERLING
Music by KERRY MILLS

When Lou-is came home to the flat,_____ He hung up his
The dress-es that hung in the hall,_____ Were gone, she had

coat and his hat,_____ He gazed all a - round, but no
tak-en them all;_____ She took all his rings and the

wif-ey he found, So he said "where can Flos-sie be at?"_____ A
rest of his things; The pic-ture he missed from the wall._____ "What!

fair,_____ Don't tell me the lights are shin-ing a - ny

place but there;_____ We will dance the Hooch - ee Kooch - ee,_____ I will

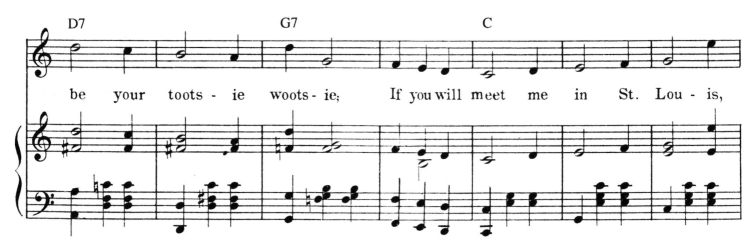

be your toots - ie woots - ie; If you will meet me in St. Lou - is,

Lou - is, Meet me at the fair!_____ fair._____

THE MERRY WIDOW WALTZ

Words by ADRIAN ROSS
Arranged for Piano by H. M. HIGGS
On Melodies by FRANZ LEHÁR

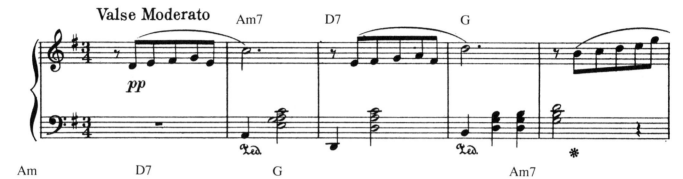

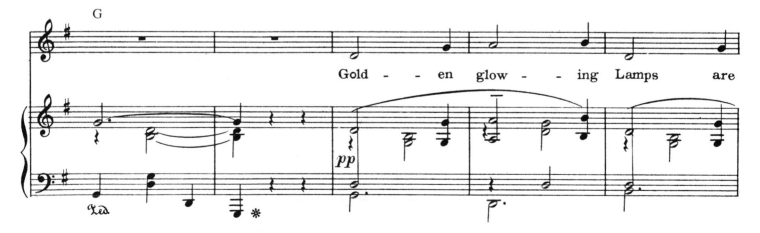

Gold - en glow - ing Lamps are

128

That seems to whisper soft and low, I love you so!

Love that hov — — ers O — — ver lov — — ers Speaks

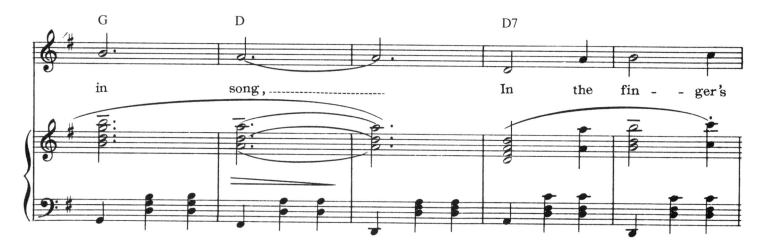

in song, In the fin — — ger's

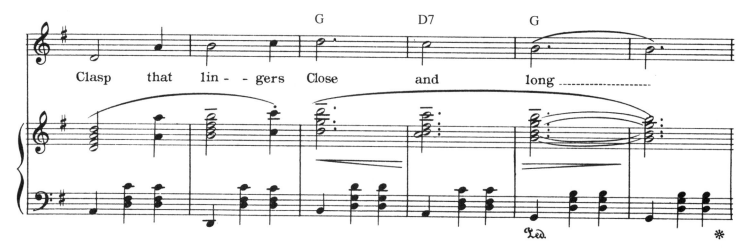

Clasp that lin — — gers Close and long

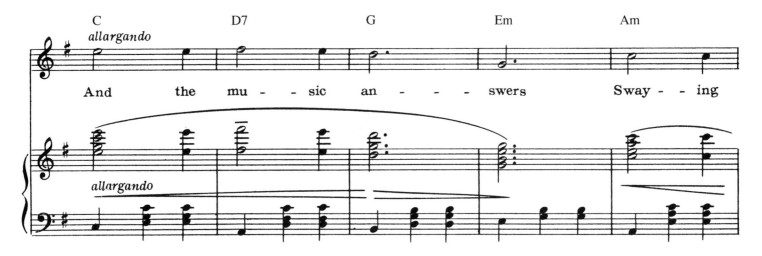

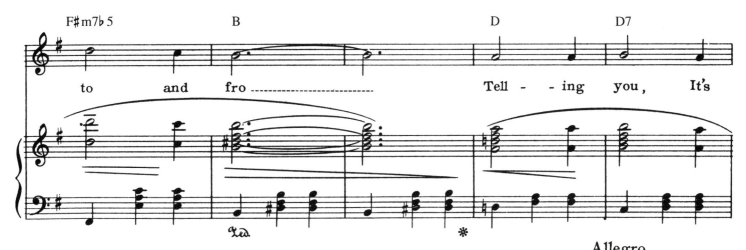

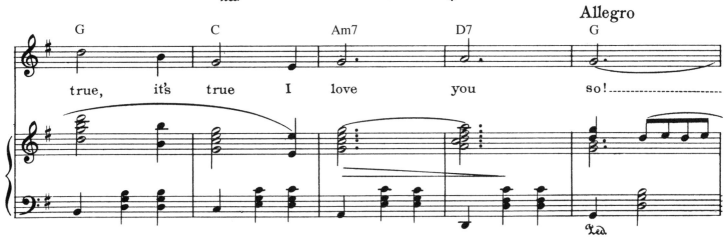

MIGHTY LAK' A ROSE

Text by FRANK L. STANTON
Music by ETHELBERT NEVIN

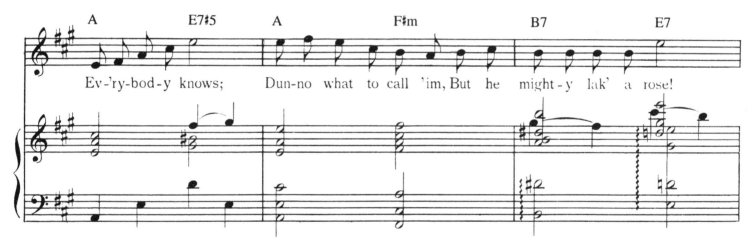

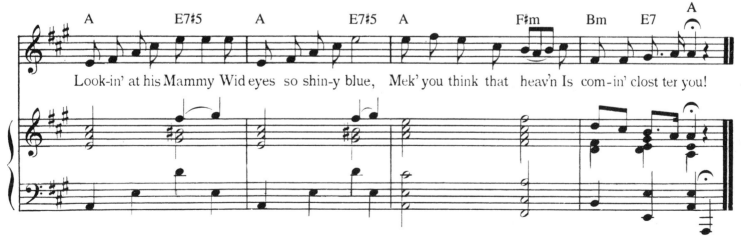

MOONBEAMS

Lyric by HENRY BLOSSOM
Music by VICTOR HERBERT

shad - ows fall in a dark - 'ning pall, And the wea - ry world's at

rest. _____ The stars are a - wak - en - ing one, by one, The

whis - per - ing breez - es are still, The moon shin - ing bright with a

ra - diant light, is sil - ver - ing val - ley and hill.

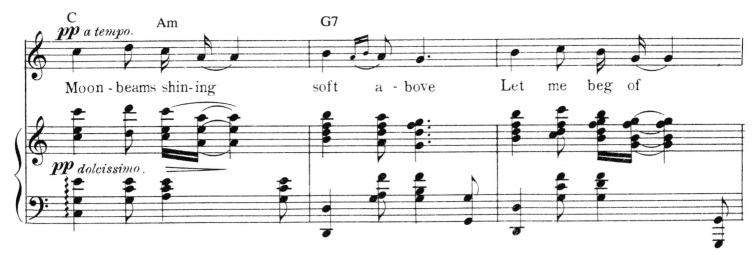

Moon-beams shin-ing soft a-bove Let me beg of

you! Find the one I dear-ly love! Tell him I'll e'er be

true. Fate may part us, years may pass!

Fut-ure all un — known! Still my love shall ev-er prove

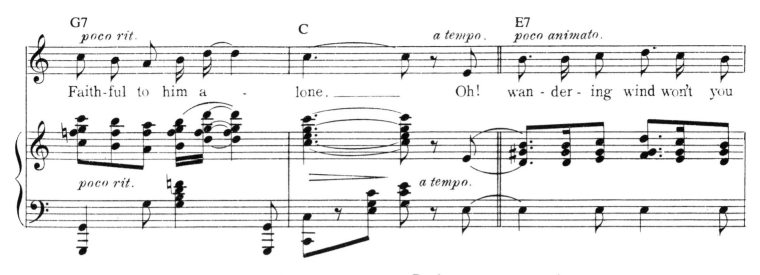

Faith-ful to him a - lone._____ Oh! wan-der-ing wind won't you

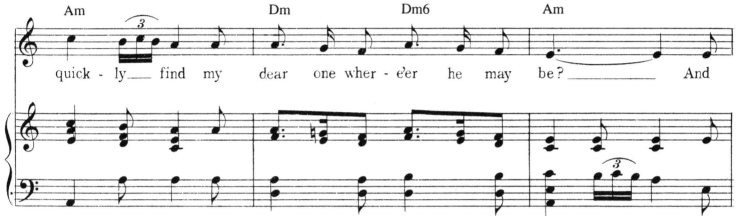

quick-ly___ find my dear one wher - e'er he may be?_____ And

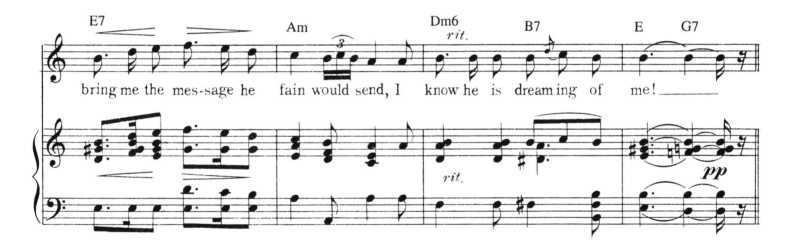

bring me the mes-sage he fain would send, I know he is dream ing of me!_____

Moon-beams shin-ing soft a - bove Let me beg of

you, Find the one I ___ dear- ly love! Tell her I'll eer be ___

true! Fate may part us, ___ years may pass,

Fut - ure all un - known! Still my love shall

ev - er prove Faith- ful to her a - lone.

ON THE ROAD TO MANDALAY

By OLEY SPEAKS
(From Kipling's "Barrack Room Ballads")

set-tin, and I know she thinks of me. For the wind is in the

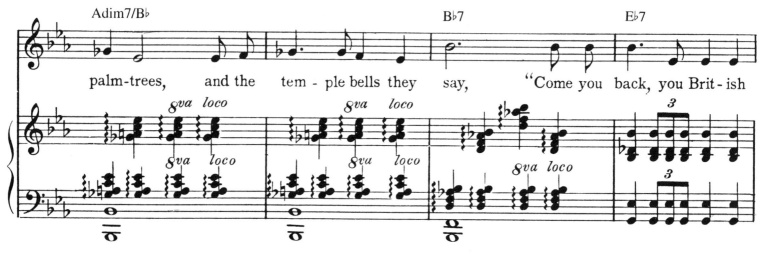

palm-trees, and the tem - ple bells they say, "Come you back, you Brit-ish

sol - dier, Come you back to Man - da - lay," Come you

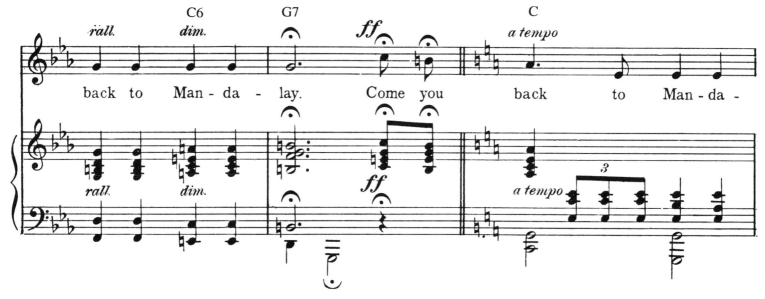

back to Man - da - lay. Come you back to Man - da -

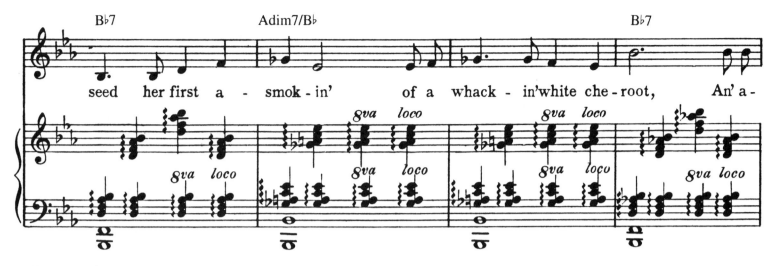

seed her first a - smok - in' of a whack - in' white che - root, An' a-

-wast - in' Chris - tian kiss - es on a 'eath - en i - dol's

foot, On a 'eath - en i - dol's foot. Bloom - in'

i - dol made o' mud, What they called the great Gawd

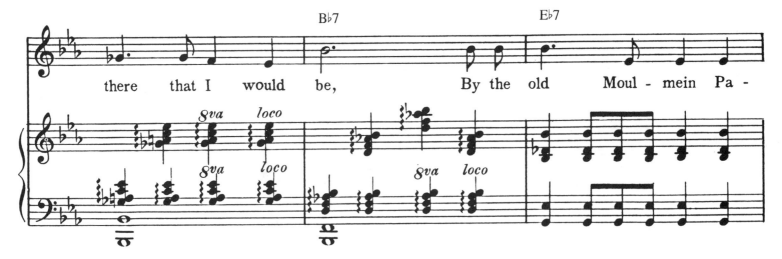

there that I would be, By the old Moul- mein Pa-

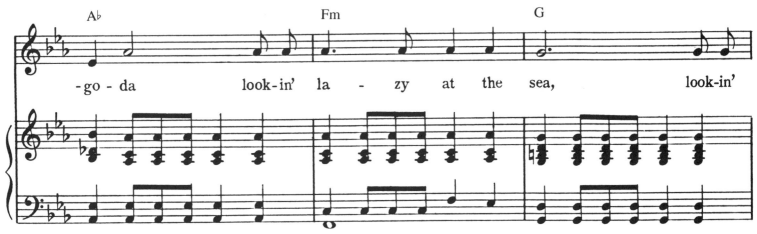

-go-da look-in' la - zy at the sea, look-in'

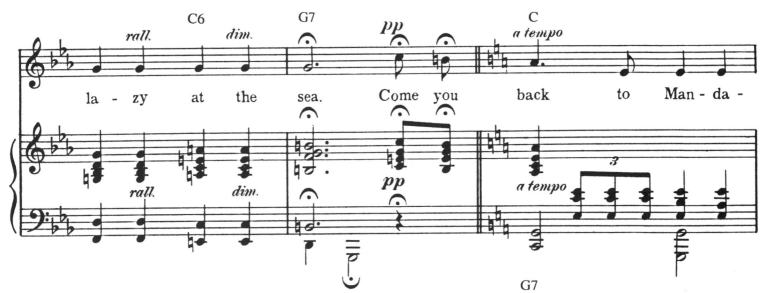

la - zy at the sea. Come you back to Man-da-

lay, where the old Flo - til - la lay, Can't you

POMP AND CIRCUMSTANCE

By SIR EDWARD ELGAR

Moderately

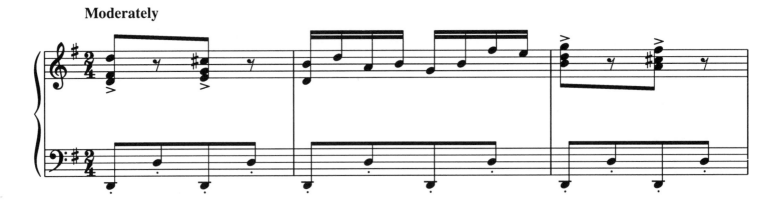

senza pedale

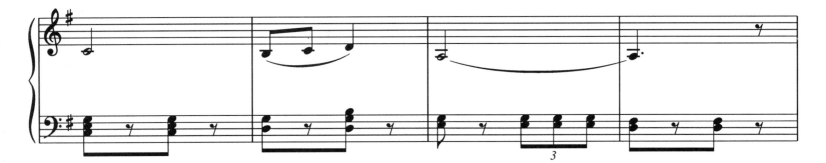

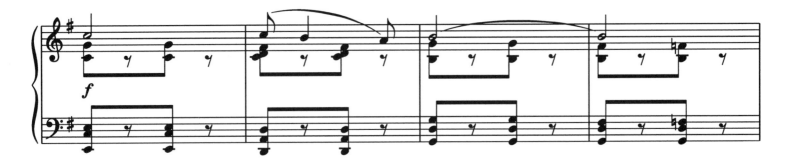

PUT ON YOUR OLD GREY BONNET

Words by STANLEY MURPHY
Music by PERCY WENRICH

On the .. old farm house ve-ran-da There sat Si-las and Mi-
It was in the same old bon-net With the same blue rib-bon

ran-da, Think-ing of the days gone by. _____ Said he
on it, In the old shay, by his side, _____ That he

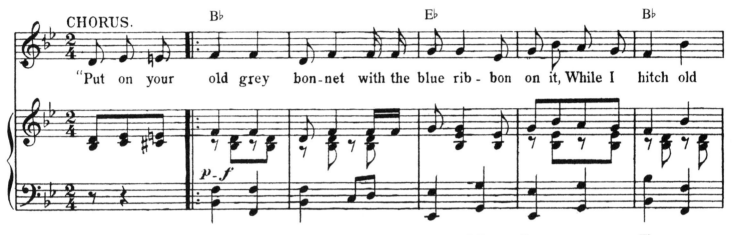

SCHOOL DAYS

By COBB & EDWARDS

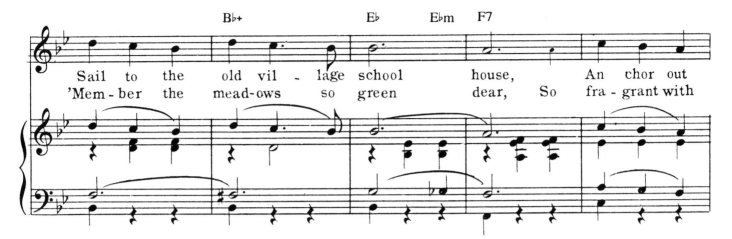

Sail to the old vil - lage school house, An chor out
'Mem - ber the mead-ows so green dear, So fra - grant with

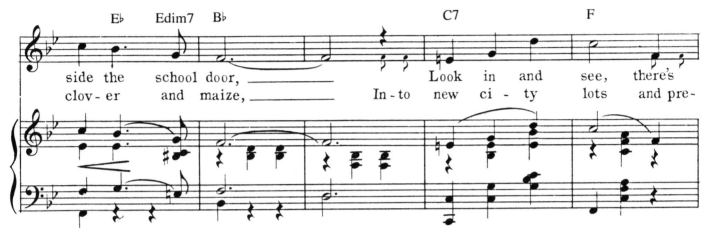

side the school door, _____ Look in and see, there's
clov - er and maize, _____ In - to new ci - ty lots and pre -

you and there's me, A coup-le of kids once more. _____
ferred bus²-ness plots, They've cut them up since those days. _____

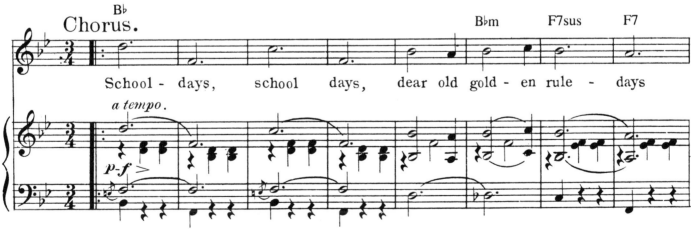

Chorus.

School - days, school days, dear old gold - en rule - days

Read - in' and 'rit - in' and 'rith - me - tic, Taught to the tune of a hick - ry

stick, You were my queen in cal - i - co, I was your

bash - ful bare - foot beau, And you wrote on my slate, I love you

Joe, When we were a coup - le of kids._____ kids._____

D.C.

SHE IS MA DAISY

Words by HARRY LAUDER and J. D. HARPER
Music by HARRY LAUDER

CHORUS

She is ma Dai - sy!.............. ma bon-nie Dai - sy!......

She's as sweet as su - gar - can - dy And she's

ver - y fond of San- dy, And I wea - ry..............

for ma dear - ie.............. I would

ra - ther lose ma whip than lose ma Dai - sy! She is ma -sy!

Fine.

D.S.

SHINE ON HARVEST MOON

Words by JACK NORWORTH
Music by NORA BAYES-NORWORTH

STOP YER TICKLING, JOCK!

Words by HARRY LAUDER and FRANK FOLLOY
Music by HARRY LAUDER

Oh! I'm court-ing a far-mer's doch-ter, She's
Oh! she went to the sea-side with me, I
Oh! I went to the farm, one Sun-day, Be-
Oh! I'm think-ing of get-ting mar-ried, In

one of the nic-est ev-er seen. Her cheeks they are a
thought she would like to see. the sea. Oh! I did en-joy my
cause she in-vit-ed me to tea. Her fai-ther and her
that, d'ye ken, there'll be no harm. Oh! be-cause I think she's

164

SWEET ADELINE

Words by RICHARD H. GERARD
Music by HENRY W. ARMSTRONG

SUNBONNET SUE

Lyric by WILL D. COBB
Melody by GUS EDWARDS

CHORUS. *Slowly - tenderly.*

Sun-bon-net Sue, Sun-bon-net Sue, Sunshine and ros-es ran sec-ond to you;

You looked so nice, I kissed you twice, Un-der your sun-bon-net blue.___ It was

on-ly a kind of a "kid kiss,"___ But it tas-ted lots nic-er than pie;___ And the

next thing I knew, I was dead stuck on you, When I was a kid so high.___ high.___

TAKE ME OUT TO THE BALL GAME

Words by JACK NORWORTH
Music by ALBERT VON TILZER

TELL ME PRETTY MAIDEN

By LESLIE STUART

(GIRLS.) There are a
(MEN.) There are a

(MEN.) Tell me, pret-ty maid-en, Are there a-ny more at home like you?
(GIRLS.) Tell me, gen-tle stran-ger Are there a-ny more at home like you?

few, kind sir, But sim-ple girls, and pro-per too.
few, sweet maid And bet-ter boys you nev-er know

Then
Then

tell me, pret-ty maid-en, What these ver-y sim-ple girl-ies do. Then
tell me, gen-tle sir, The things these ver-y rak-ish fel-lows do. Then

man-ner are per-fec-tion, And the op-po-site of mine.
flirt with girls too free-ly And it's not the same girl twice.

tell me, maid-en, what the girl - ies do, Then take a lit-tle
tell me, tell me what these fel - lows do, Then take me 'round and

walk with me, And then I can see What a most par-tic-u-lar girl should be.
let them show for an hour or so How far such fel-lows can real-ly___ go.

must love some one, real-ly And it might as well be you!
must love some one, real-ly And it might as well be you!

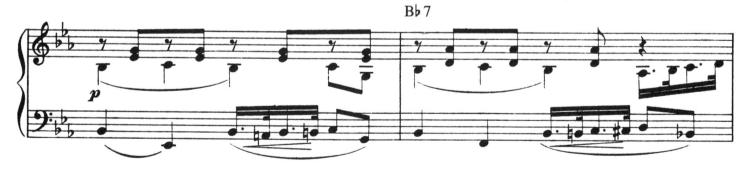

TOYLAND

Lyric by GLEN MAC DONOUGH
Music by VICTOR HERBERT

UNDER THE BAMBOO TREE

By BOB COLE

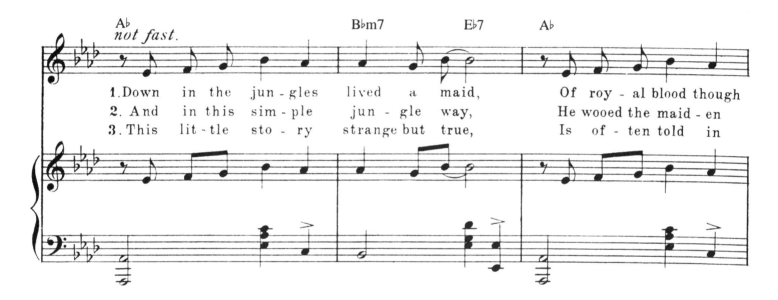

1. Down in the jun-gles lived a maid, Of roy-al blood though
2. And in this sim-ple jun-gle way, He wooed the maid-en
3. This lit-tle sto-ry strange but true, Is of-ten told in

dus-ky shade, A marked im-pres-sion once she made
ev'-ry day, By sing-ing what he had to say;
Ma-ta-boo, Of how this Zu-lu tried to woo

Up-on a Zu-lu / from Ma-ta-boo-loo; / And ev'-ry morning
One day he seized her / and gen-tly squeezed her; / And then be-neath the
His jun-gle la-dy / in tropics sha-dy; / Al-though the scene was

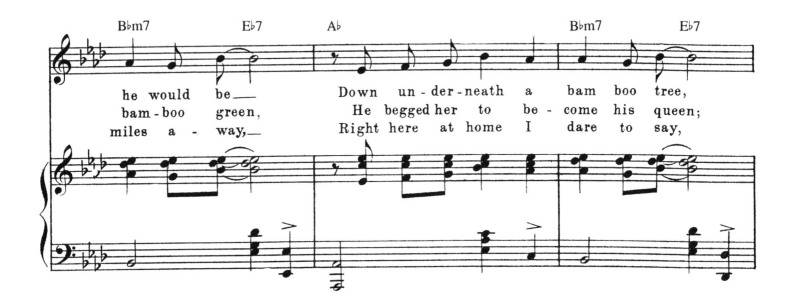

he would be___ / Down un-der-neath a bam boo tree,
bam-boo green, / He begged her to be-come his queen;
miles a-way,___ / Right here at home I dare to say,

A-wait-ing there his love to see / And then to her he'd sing:___
The dus-ky maid-en blushed un-seen / And joined him in his song.___
You'll hear some Zu-lu ev'-ry day, / Gush out this soft re-frain:___

Chorus. *not fast*.

If you lak-a-me, lak I lak-a-you And we lak-a-both the

same, I lak-a say, this ve-ry day, I lak-a-change your name; 'Cause

I love-a-you and love-a-you true And if you-a love-a-me.

One live as two, two live as one Un-der the bam-boo tree. If tree.

VILIA

Words by ADRIAN ROSS
Music by FRANZ LEHAR
Arranged for the Piano by H. M. HIGGS

Allegretto

There once was a Vil - ia, A witch of the wood, A hunt - er be-held her a - lone as she stood. The spell of her beau - ty up-

Allegretto

The wood-maid-en smiled, and no an - swer she gave, But beck-on'd him in - - to the shade of the cave; He nev - - er had known such a rap - tur - ous bliss, No maid - en of mor - tals so sweet - ly can kiss!

WAIT TILL THE SUN SHINES, NELLIE

Words by ANDREW B. STERLING
Music by HARRY VON TILZER

On a Sun-day Morn, sat a maid for-lorn,__ With her
"How I long," she sighed, "for a trol-ley ride,__ Just to

sweet-heart by__ her side;____ Thro' the win-dow pane, she looked
show my brand new gown,"__ Then she gazed on high with a

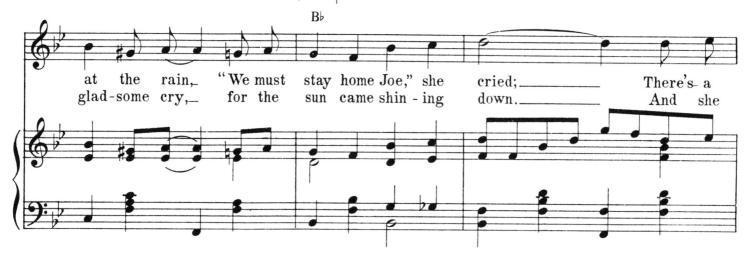

at the rain, "We must stay home Joe," she cried;____ There's a
glad-some cry,__ for the sun came shin-ing down.__ And she

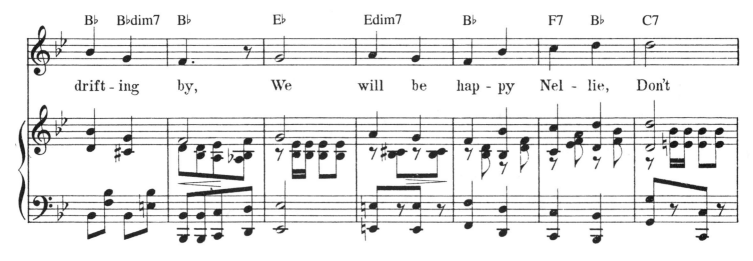

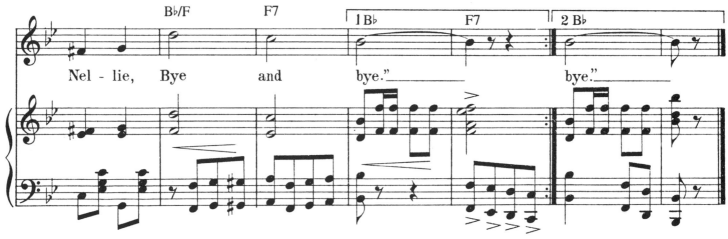

WHAT YOU GOIN' TO DO
WHEN THE RENT COMES 'ROUND?

Words by ANDREW B. STERLING
Music by HARRY VON TILZER

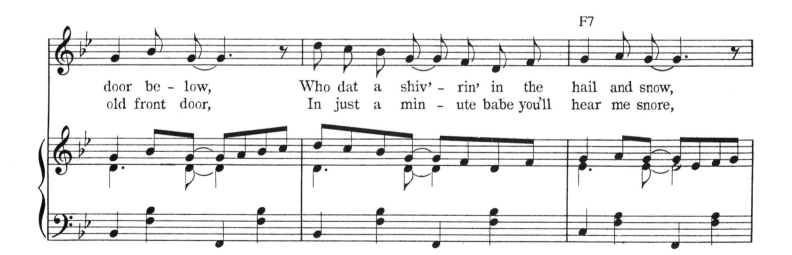

I can hear you grumblin' Mis-ter Ru-fus Brown,   Just keep on a-knock-in' babe, I
If I goes to bed with-out a bite or sup,   You will be an i - ci - cle when

won't come down,   I wants to tell you that you can't get in,
I wakes up,   Where's all the mon - ey that you said you'd bring,

Have you been a gamblin' Hon-ey, did you win?   what's that you tell me Hon
Mel-ted all a-way just like the snow last Spring,   Ru-fus I loves you, but

you lost your breath?   I hopes you freez - es to death.___
this serves you right,   Guess that's suf - fi - cient, "Good - night."___

YANKEE DOODLE BOY
(A/K/A I'M A YANKEE DOODLE DANDY)

Tempo di Marcia.

By GEORGE M. COHAN

I'm the kid that's all the can - dy,
Fa - ther's name was Hez - i - ki - ah,

I'm a Yan - kee Doo - dle Dan - dy, I'm glad I am,___
Moth - er's name was Ann Ma - ri - a, Yanks through and through.

200

that ain't a josh, She's a Yan - kee, by gosh. *CHO.*(Oh,
that's go - ing some, For the Yan - kees, by gum. *CHO.*(Oh,

say   can you   see _____ An - y -
say   can you   see _____ An - y -

thing a - bout a Yan - kee that's a phon - - ey?)
thing a - bout my ped - i - gree that's phon - - ey?)

CHORUS.

I'm a Yan-kee Doo-dle Dan - dy, A Yan - kee Doo-dle, do or die; A real live nep-hew of my Un - cle Sam's, Born on the Fourth of Ju - ly. I've

YIP-I-ADDY-I-AY!

Words by WILL D. COBB
Music by JNO. H. FLYNN

night he saw danc-ing, a maid so en-tranc-ing, His heart caught on
look not Spring Val-ley, to wel-come home Sal-ly, Who went to New
played and she tar-ried, that night they "got" mar-ried, But ev-en be-

fi-re in-side,_____ And mus-ic so mel-low he
York for the ride;_____ For the night that Von Bel-low cut
fore break of day,_____ Poor sleep-y Von Bel-low, heard

sawed on his cel-lo, She waltzed up to him and she cried:_____
loose on his cel-lo, She tore up her tick-et and cried:_____
his new wife yell-oh,"For good-ness sake, wake up and play!_____

CHORUS.

E__Yip - I - Ad-dy-I - Ay, - I - Ay! E__Yip - I - Ad-dy-I -

YOU'RE A GRAND OLD FLAG

Words and Music by
GEORGE M. COHAN

Lyrics:
You're a grand old flag. You're a high fly-ing flag and for-ev-er in peace may you wave. You're the em-blem of the land I love, the home of the free and the

THE DECADE SERIES

The Decade Series explores the music of the 1890's to the 1980's through each era's major events and personalities. Each volume features text and photos and over 40 of the decade's top songs, so readers can see how music has acted as a mirror or a catalyst for current events and trends. Each book is arranged for piano, voice & guitar.

Songs Of The 1890's
Over 50 songs, including: America, The Beautiful • The Band Played On • Hello! Ma Baby • Maple Leaf Rag • My Wild Irish Rose • O Sole Mio • The Sidewalks Of New York • The Stars And Stripes Forever • Ta Ra Ra Boom De Ay • Who Threw The Overalls In Mistress Murphy's Chowder • and more.

_____00311655 ....$12.95

Songs Of The 1900s – 1900-1909
Over 50 favorites, including: Anchors Aweigh • Bill Bailey, Won't You Please Come Home • By The Light Of The Silvery Moon • Fascination • Give My Regards To Broadway • Mary's A Grand Old Name • Meet Me In St. Louis • Shine On Harvest Moon • Sweet Adeline • Take Me Out to the Ball Game • Waltzing Matilda • The Yankee Doodle Boy • You're A Grand Old Flag • and more.

_____00311656 ....$12.95

Songs Of The 1910s
Over 50 classics, including: After You've Gone • Alexander's Ragtime Band • Danny Boy • (Back Home Again) In Indiana • Let Me Call You Sweetheart • My Melancholy Baby • 'Neath The Southern Moon • Oh, You Beautiful Doll • Rock-A-Bye Your Baby With A Dixie Melody • When Irish Eyes Are Smiling • You Made Me Love You • and more.

_____00311657 ....$12.95

Songs Of The 20's
58 songs, featuring: Ain't Misbehavin' • April Showers • Baby Face • California Here I Come • Five Foot Two, Eyes Of Blue • I Can't Give You Anything But Love • Manhattan • Stardust • The Varsity Drag • Who's Sorry Now.

_____00361122 ....$14.95

Songs Of The 30's
61 songs, featuring: All Of Me • The Continental • I Can't Get Started • I'm Getting Sentimental Over You • In The Mood • The Lady Is A Tramp • Love Letters In The Sand • My Funny Valentine • Smoke Gets In Your Eyes • What A Diff'rence A Day Made.

_____00361123 ....$14.95

Songs Of The 40's
61 songs, featuring: Come Rain Or Come Shine • God Bless The Child • How High The Moon • The Last Time I Saw Paris • Moonlight In Vermont • A Nightingale Sang In Berkeley Square • A String Of Pearls • Swinging On A Star • Tuxedo Junction • You'll Never Walk Alone.

_____00361124 ....$14.95

Songs Of The 50's
59 songs, featuring: Blue Suede Shoes • Blue Velvet • Here's That Rainy Day • Love Me Tender • Misty • Rock Around The Clock • Satin Doll • Tammy • Three Coins In The Fountain • Young At Heart.

_____00361125 ....$14.95

Songs Of The 60's
60 songs, featuring: By The Time I Get To Phoenix • California Dreamin' • Can't Help Falling In Love • Downtown • Green Green Grass Of Home • Happy Together • I Want To Hold Your Hand • Love Is Blue • More • Strangers In The Night.

_____00361126 ....$14.95

Songs Of The 70's
More than 45 songs including: Don't Cry For Me Argentina • Feelings • The First Time Ever I Saw Your Face • How Deep Is Your Love • Imagine • Let It Be • Me And Bobby McGee • Piano Man • Reunited • Send In The Clowns • Sometimes When We Touch • Tomorrow • You Don't Bring Me Flowers • You Needed Me.

_____00361127 ....$14.95

Songs Of The 80's
Over 40 of this decade's biggest hits, including: Candle In The Wind • Don't Worry, Be Happy • Ebony And Ivory • Endless Love • Every Breath You Take • Flashdance... What A Feeling • Islands In The Stream • Kokomo • Memory • Sailing • Somewhere Out There • We Built This City • What's Love Got To Do With It • With Or Without You.

_____00490275 ....$14.95

MORE SONGS OF THE DECADE SERIES

Due to popular demand, we are pleased to present these new collections with even more great songs from the 1920s through 1980s. Each book features piano/vocal/guitar arrangements. Perfect for practicing musicians, educators, collectors, and music hobbyists.

More Songs Of The '20s
Over 50 songs, including: Ain't We Got Fun? • All By Myself • Bill • Carolina In The Morning • Fascinating Rhythm • The Hawaiian Wedding Song • I Want To Be Bad • I'm Just Wild About Harry • Malagueña • Nobody Knows You When You're Down And Out • Someone To Watch Over Me • Yes, Sir, That's My Baby • and more.

_____00311647 ....$14.95

More Songs of the '30s
Over 50 songs, including: All The Things You Are • Begin The Beguine • A Fine Romance • I Only Have Eyes For You • In A Sentimental Mood • Just A Gigolo • Let's Call The Whole Thing Off • The Most Beautiful Girl In The World • Mad Dogs And Englishmen • Stompin' At The Savoy • Stormy Weather • Thanks For The Memory • The Very Thought Of You • and more.

_____00311648 ....$14.95

More Songs Of The '40s
Over 60 songs, including: Bali Ha'i • Be Careful, It's My Heart • A Dream Is A Wish Your Heart Makes • Five Guys Named Moe • Is You Is, Or Is You Ain't (Ma' Baby) • The Last Time I Saw Paris • Old Devil Moon • San Antonio Rose • Some Enchanted Evening • Steppin' Out With My Baby • Take The "A" Train • Too Darn Hot • Zip-A-Dee-Doo-Dah • and more.

_____00311649 ....$14.95

More Songs Of The '50s
Over 50 songs, including: All Of You • Blueberry Hill • Chanson D'Amour • Charlie Brown • Do-Re-Mi • Hey, Good Lookin' • Hound Dog • I Could Have Danced All Night • Love And Marriage • Mack The Knife • Mona Lisa • My Favorite Things • Sixteen Tons • (Let Me Be Your) Teddy Bear • That's Amore • Yakety Yak • and more.

_____00311650 ....$14.95

More Songs Of The '60s
Over 60 songs, including: Alfie • Baby Elephant Walk • Bonanza • Born To Be Wild • Eleanor Rigby • The Impossible Dream • Leaving On A Jet Plane • Moon River • Raindrops Keep Fallin' On My Head • Ruby, Don't Take Your Love To Town • Seasons In The Sun • Sweet Caroline • Tell Laura I Love Her • A Time For Us • What The World Needs Now • Wooly Bully • and more.

_____00311651 ....$14.95

More Songs Of The '70s
Over 50 songs, including: Afternoon Delight • All By Myself • American Pie • Billy, Don't Be A Hero • The Candy Man • Happy Days • I Shot The Sheriff • Long Cool Woman (In A Black Dress) • Maggie May • On Broadway • She Believes In Me • She's Always A Woman • Spiders And Snakes • Star Wars • Taxi • You've Got A Friend • and more.

_____00311652 ....$14.95

More Songs Of The '80s
Over 50 songs, including: Addicted To Love • Almost Paradise • Axel F • Call Me • Don't Know Much • Even The Nights Are Better • Footloose • Funkytown • Girls Just Want To Have Fun • The Heat Is On • Karma Chameleon • Longer • Straight Up • Take My Breath Away • Tell Her About It • We're In This Love Together • and more.

_____00311653 ....$14.95

FOR MORE INFORMATION, SEE YOUR LOCAL MUSIC DEALER, OR WRITE TO:

HAL•LEONARD

7777 W. BLUEMOUND RD. P.O. BOX 13819 MILWAUKEE, WI 53213

Prices, availability & contents subject to change without notice.